November 2022

Bloom

For Christina -
Lovely to meet you
through eco-poetry -
may your poems flourish
+ grow -

Sarah Westcott

v

Bloom

Sarah Westcott

First published 2021 by
Liverpool University Press
4 Cambridge Street
Liverpool
L69 7ZU

British Library Cataloguing-in-Publication data
A British Library CIP record is available

ISBN 978-1-800-34870-7 softback

Typeset by Carnegie Book Production, Lancaster
Printed and bound in Poland by Booksfactory.co.uk

& when we have planted flowers
& talked into the ears of our dogs, let us go back

Aracelis Girmay, *Litany*

Contents

Apples

Have you looked,
have you looked deeply —

the *feeling*,
the feeling is what I mean.

I look at Marina looking at Ulay and I look at myself and we brim.

*

I hold a dove and look into its ringed eye. Its body is a trembling boat. I am in and out of my self. I see my face – small floating Narcissus, a ring of iris etched in dark. The bird returns my gaze with difference. Its organs are lit meat. I fall into   ———,   the space around stars, my mind a weaned point of light.

*

I look into the eyes of my dog and it is a violent act. The dog eye is a landscape I cannot reach and the dog is running here. Language: a barrier, a raft of sticks, a child with a nest in his hands.

*

April: frothing and foaming,
cuckoo spit dripping from its mouth.
Cellular thrumming in wet light. Oh travellers.

It is not easy marking a blank sheet. It is privileged and
luxurious.
Fantasy moves in like bacteria. I go out to look.

*

April dead in this sentence. The leaf unfurled long before we
called it a leaf. Or blatt. Or folium. We cling to one word:
health.

I wear language as a skin, I shed it at night. I lie in bed, a
child with loose hair and I forget everything.

I wake, I wear language as a skin. I speak only one with
words. Words laid down under those from the future,
scratches and indentations.

*

Sometimes I look at trees. I think about the providence of wood for humans. It floats, burns, weathers, bears weight, is pliable and solid. See also grass: oh most practical coir. Make us a poultice, soak it with milk.

*

I sometimes feel close to the place we come from before birth. The sense is clear and deep, like deep sea water, fatal and blankly colossal. Fill my mouth with thick light.

*

I used to try and make things move by the power of thought. Stare at them, my thoughts a split beam. I could not make the apple roll.
Can you see it rolling?
A small green point coming towards you, a sweet green sphere.

Man

It starts in water, like everything.
All beginnings are naive.
When he rises above me

he holds my leg and moves himself
on its strength
like a drowning man.

He is silent but his face
holds all the weathers.
I sing a song so tiny

he holds me, trembling
and brings me to his face.
I do not know where to look

when he walks towards me.
It is beginning to rain:
strange, tangible, fair.

Night comes,
arresting, hinged thing,
a moth, lobed, in the brocade.

I dream of two white egrets,
a parent and a chick,
the English dirt up their fronts.

How might we end?
With all the blandness of any beginning,
municipal, descant.

Ring

This tender little child
gave up enough flesh
to make a circlet of ring.

A wing of skin, nicked
and slipped over her finger.

His tiny glans
a bleeding line,
crossed and forgotten.

A little piece of skin
alike the skin in an egg.

His bride wore yellow.
Her dress was wings of goldfinch.

Boy

They are nailing him into the wood
And I don't know what to do.

I think about him dying,
The cross and the crossing,

The pelmet of his shoulder soft
Against the wood, the fingers

Limp and beautiful, a nick
On his thumb from a thorn.

Boy, bleeding for all the songs
Of the birds pinned into his breath.

What am I trying to say? Let us go
To the crops now, and bear these feelings.

Desert Holly

I collected a plant from the garden of a mass shooter,
a desert holly with grey leaves,
and moved some pieces of earth.

I cultivated a forest clearing
nurtured by re-tweets,
every mouth was ringing.

I filmed a bird driving
(the loneliest bird in the shop).
we drove to the Salton Sea –

he held the wheel with his feet,
the mice played Art Garfunkel
on their wheels in the cage.

I grew trees through the roof of my car,
the fruit rolled down and I ate some –

I grew grapes on rugs in a castle,
we were ruinous.

I grew corn for a plant concert –
our heads were levelled pipes and organs.

I released three flies in a mall,
in the moments of leaving they were blue, gold and green —
I had in mind clean shadows,
        they touched my face like a child.

Iron Baby

Sleeping, or not crying,
life-size newborn
cast from the artist's daughter,
six days old.

Comfort in fist to mouth,
her head laid on concrete
in full-blooded dream.

Who could leave a baby
alone, naked,
who could walk past?

I want to kiss her cheek,
taste the blood and salt,
the tang of where she passed.

Gathering, what does she gather?
Body curled,
knees touching arms —

let me hold her,
too heavy to bear,
gobbet, clove, kernel, bomb —

none of these,
a baby cast in solid iron,
her fist at her mouth, o comfort.

Light falls almost-green upon her back,
baby/non-baby
softly, softly,
we open our arms.

Breast

All night he's on me like a lamb
and it is a love act, this feeding
fit to his wet mouth, his baby guts,
sucked neat from the heart.

How do we make it, this sweetness?
Through the light of an old moon
the rain throws stones
the sleeping have no need to hear.

He of the old place, old be,
He snores into himself, slow clock unwinding,
I hear his heart like an old cello hollow
and the little dog heart going down by the door.

O low He snores and lo the little he
sucks for the living thirst of us all –

What-what-what tongue is he taking,
swallowing me, my mother, anon,
what matter is he gobbling
in the hours where the mild are loud
and lack shrieks us awake in the morning?

Pigeons

A collared bird is drinking –
it bows to the river,
water wets its crop.

Dreaming has always moved
in the skin of the river,
the voiceless river, all throat.

We granted a river
the same rights as human –
empathy, care, compassion.

Words meet water and run
with muddy meaning,
the pigeon, light on its shoulders,

a clean answer to the body –
space emerges around its flight.
We read narratives of loss,

remember feathered napes
dove-grey, peach and gold,
trees shaken by a living wind

the body of each bird, very private.
Wings are laced with sentiment
empathy is sweet to bear,

liquid running over feathers
small bodies of water
dying away into water –

how to fade from
the wheeling optics,
would you like to see everything all at once?

Pool

You saw your reflection once
at the bottom of a cup,
recognised the child wavering
at the edge of the pool.

The water there is colourless
or all colours, not yet split
by the greedy eye.
You bend to it and drink.

Beauty

I wanted my hands to touch something alive,
picked daisies, celandine, forget-me-not and bluebell –
behind the ears they were a blue haze.
The bluebell held six petals curling upwards,
a cute and inaccurate octopus, a lifted kilt,
a bell of soft lead a child might shape into a flower head.
The celandines opened startled faces,
their yellow-green hearts pushed into the air.
The forget-me-nots were the back of my wrist,
a deep summer of being sixteen and running out
into a morning when form and perception were, once, the same.

To hold loss in our bodies

If I sit here long enough I hear the gulls, knives turned in the light. Tawny, blue and gold; the lake is patient. Some peace holds memories of ague, marshed lives. A woman in a dark dress, child on her back. Unknown child of the near past. Birds watching and listening, always. Old shapes persisting, old rooms. It is difficult to write of this, it is the easiest thing in the world to think the lake's blue skin, the unloved bricks and fallen posts, a crust of birds on the rim. Nothing is deliberate but everything is also. Nothing to be told but light. I keep myself tucked away as an egg's contents, or a bladder's gold hoard. Radiant birds, what longing sets them circling, where do their bodies leave us, when we cannot hear them anymore? I hear what I can hear, weepings and softenings without interpretation or layer.

Spring Fragments

25th March

Time, sifted through the hands.
Time remaining: grains, grits, particles,
hard measures.

Time at the window rubbing its striped rump
at the glass or singing, its pink mouth open,
sliding down the panes.

Time the life of a leaf, feathery with flower –
an absurd catkin.

Time deepening and loosening, leaf fado
stewed into the richness,
itself the richness.

*

How dependent we are on the light,
how quiet the streets

death in the bright, clear skies
unabashed light falling on our heads

the air we inspire
is nothing more than one person away

I see one aeroplane
the contrails break into genetic code

chromosomes opening into further forms
up the cow parsley comes

I pick a crust of lichen off the roof
try to inhabit two truths at once

Wednesday afternoon

A quiet, still grey cup.
Dove-grey,
dove-grey the content –
limpid, pensive, creamed.
So abstracted! Light comes; blue-tint.

29th March

Everyone inside like eggs

soft, wet egg-in-the-shell
sliding up and down smooth insides.

A man's face is shaved so cleanly
it is smooth as an egg and expressionless.

31st March

The wound of each hour
Blossom at our feet is bright
Foaming from the graves

4th April

My son, pesto-breath
All my other selves piled up
Swatches on a spike

8th April

every evening
the light is different
today it is paste
milky, sieved,
gentle persistent
very beautiful

alveoli slowly
swelling
with light

I lift my face
insects batter at the glass
the lightest branches move with the wind

16th April

Lunchtime; the street came out of our homes and stood and clapped as the widower was helped into a car and driven away.

18th April

My menstrual cycle, stolid and flowering. Two wheels, or three, turning.

More flowers: (a)biding.

26th April

Tonight I am the buttercups
Somewhat
Faded and shiny

They have drunk:
I did not see if they opened
To the daylight,

They are singular and vivid, all self
Or none at all

When I smell them
I can only smell myself

Some date in April

Red damselfly, still in the sun. Long, flopping body. Walnut in flower with long, extended catkins. My breasts as I walk. Outlines of bodies under cloth. The sound of bicycle wheels louder than cars. Birds are quiet, feeding their young; incessant attention! An egg tooth taps, insistent, until I feel myself breaking through. I think of arms like catkins, I think of keys, of tiny fetishisations, of undistinguished things: seeds, waterbuts, palpable concerns.

*

Drawing a Sunflower

Each day I wake into a yellow entity,
the central disc is textured
with hooks –
a density of expression.

The yellow flames are a decoy.
The dark disc is energy,
investment, blind investment
in this mode of holding.

The leaves are easier,
a little tattered,
their shape in the pen
almost water.
Put me down again
upon on the earth
(more resistance in the paper).

Dream cell

I could hear breathing and it was not my own. I held my breath and the breathing went on beyond me, a stream. I started to breathe again and I could hear my heart and lungs, faithful. I woke into myself in the small single bed of my body, I woke into the white, not-white light, an inflorescence. There were no eyes and it was terrible. I went out into my body then, and I lived it.

*

Some date in April

A box of blue tits, sly and secretive, an ear on the side of our lives. Chicks with gluey mouths. I dare not lift the roof, break in.

The babies call as adulthood breaks in their pin bones.
I can hear them through the walls.

We intersect on the wires, the glass an instrument we both play.
I write across the glass with my eyes, some dolour, some longings.

Their cries are little stabs, pure and high. Setting their arrows into the air.
The plants put their mouths down the sides of the hills.

29th April

A clear, bright, late day. We walk before my child sleeps. I remember the wooden cross in the church grounds with a crown of barbed wire. We approach it across wet grass – the shape is atavistic – four points like a body – the raised head and still legs. I think my son cannot tell between real cross and apocryphal. I think we all enjoy entering these uncertainties.

Under the cross are dog violets in various stages of growth. I take three to study at home. I put my glasses on – there is a pale, striped opening in the middle lower petal, the stripes like veins in the back of the throat, drawn by the cell's inheritance, leading in to the back of the slipper, the heel, the spur which when pinched is surprisingly firm.

Some day in May

I must bear with myself
& these field flowers;
daisies, simple violets.

I will sing
daisies, violets,
poppies' crushed light.

I close my eyes
to all the children
in the flowers.

I hear them crying
in the trees,
my breasts ache,
drip into thin mouths.

1st May

A cuckoo, soft and plaintive, eternal and plaintive, two-toned
woody fallings, counter-balanced, strange.

*

2nd May

First swifts in grey skies, windblown and fine. The familiar
heart-strung joy. They are quiet and feed steadily, fill their
crops with beasts of air.

I hear two ice cream vans. People line up for B&Q, carry
decking paint and oil to their cars.

The clouds have been wild, bilious and changeable, we dress,
undress, dress our skins.

Today I saw a man and woman in the woods, and the man
walked up to an ancient oak and kissed its trunk like he was
kissing his mother.

*

Mid-life

There are parts of our bodies we will never know.

The soul, animate,

needs a body to rove in the animal way
as buds split with the violence of dawn.

What do we do to each other? That we cannot do to
ourselves

in the soft-locked rooms of our bodies,
       such ministrations –
                        dear bodies we grub for you
in the dark soil, the dark beds, where children wait for
mothers —

                    *

I hold a robin, eyes filling with cloud,
ribbed soft breast —

What last song did it put in the air?
    Our last words are coming,
buds splitting their song   sweet mercy of our bodies
falling open.

Old man's beard (wild clematis)

Swan among the flowers, sweet-bent

overhanging a bower or slack chin
(even in death it holds)
the little folly, damp and ivy-dark.

Hair as comfort,
hair as alternative texture,
as a strong-man strains
to lift the barbell and the hair inside him quivers.

Only winter can change it, and marginally.

Bud

Tapered, some economy.
Between the twists an opening,
promise of a line.

bloom [menarche]

come the flowers
from our bodies,
showing their faces –

such delicate shapes
red-tipped,
terrible –

first spring flowers
slit and stalked,
bathed in holy water.

Fair Maids of February

Little milk flower
trembling in the first light
barely a cotton skirt
its ragged hem almost elegant –

So many of you this morning!
White headscarves drawn tight
over the quiet graves
all wormy and downy –

Sweetest girls,
under the ivy and yew
tend your tapered
lives with light.

O suffer the little children –
their faces in the darkest hours
on street corners, under lights,
their lovely necks bowed.

The Walled Garden

A walled garden is a closed ecosystem in which all operations are controlled by the ecosystem operator. A double wall of outer stone with brick interior creates microclimates where tender organisms can grow. In my country, there is a walled garden called Kwangmyong. Users are unable to escape unless the walls are taken down. Airborne creatures can fly in or out but there is no pollen, and seeds are rare. One morning I climbed the stone wall and looked in at the green, green garden. There were rows of vegetable leaves, butterflies lit with eyes, beds of bright flowers. The smell of sweet peas was bewildering. I decided to make this garden my own. I play on a red swing and every autumn ripe apples fall from the trees. Some day I will build a wall around my garden to protect it. Once you build a wall you cannot take it down because its shadow stays. My garden is unlike Kwangmyong. I have been known to gorge myself on radish and lettuce until I feel quite deliriously unwell. There is so much living in my garden; an unbelievable variety of snail, frog and bat. There are more creatures in the soil than above it. I would like you to come and visit. I am making a gold plaque for the bench; it reads: in memory of happy hours I dreamt of spending here –

Deflower

My head was full of flowers –
    White blossom
Flowers fell from my lips,
    Sour sap
Fizzing on my teeth.

Apple blossom sang
    High notes
Into my liver –
    Sweet, white flowers
Sweet, sour night.

You laid your body over mine –
    I was a pressed flower
Tissue opening
    In your hands,
White blossom falling.

You pulled a small wild flower
    From between my legs,
Tugged its long root
    Out like a hair,
Sweet, sour singing.

And still the flowers grow,
    Sweet wild flowers
Filling our daughters' arms –
    Sweet, white flowers,
Apple blossom falling.

With a pure heart fervently

I cried to the lord *clear our hearts*
I went to the river for clarity

I waded into plastic –

a blunt wake closed behind me
I smelt lungs foaming
saw tears confect a mask of sufferance

For who remembers the small dead washed in salt on the shore?

For we are brought so very low
For this is too strong for us

Back there is a child – before it all locks up
and she can feel the tinge as a boy rips the wings from a fly

She runs a stream of cold clear tap water and it is beautiful

I cried to the lord
Love one another with a pure heart fervently
I didn't know what to say

For all flesh is grass
The flower of grass
It was not a clear ending

Small Rain

A cento

Last night I heard that short quick note
of birds flying in the dark:

if this should be the voice of Oedicnemus
I accuse this bird of making sad havoc.

Sky thickens with flisky clouds.
The hot bed streams very much.

A starving wigeon settled yesterday, & was taken.
Quick-set hedges begin to leaf.

I sowed the border with upright larkspurs; a fine sort.
The green woodpecker laughs in the fields of Vauxhall.

The male bloom of the cucumbers opens:
the bed is warm, & the plants thrive.

My Brother's cucumbers are strong, & healthy.
A vast snake appears at the hot beds.

Several fruit have bloom in the first bed
& all the little blandishments are open.

Love

I looked to the swifts –
        curved and deckled,

heard their screams,
     thought of feet,
crabbed and dark
        like wire.

I thought how eggs might feel
next to the skin and I thought
I might put an egg next to my skin

and were swift eggs blue or grey or speckled?
I looked up out of my body,
I was sorry
        [always saying sorry]

I saw two forms come close,
their bodies glance, press together –

    they tilted out
over rooflines and gardens,
openings
        into further flight –

what they passed
in that glancing touch
I pass to you so raggedly –

Abigail

A girl is playing chase   with the spring.
Morning has broken   pale stars & petals on the ground.
She is seven   her name: Abigail.

I want her to know we have never forgotten
her flaxen plaits & curly mouth.

I want to remember also
the boy who flew over cliffs,

the boy who when beaten barked
the woman who sank under peach bubbles
knick knacks in her room   needle in her hand.

I dream of my mother   slipping   from her body

her mother open-armed   other mothers waiting
for all the lost children   to lay their soft heads down.

Cherries

What might slip out
    through breaking skin,
what red or glistening drupes?

A body lies close
    inside my body,
flowers in the stupefied light.

Princess

A welt of bloom
    like meat, it sweetens and turns.

We lift the flowers,
    fans of stalks

and gracile heads,
    cottony burdens.

Thousands of heads
    breathing into cellophane –

bright fabrics and cultivars,
    tears for every wilted life.

I'd like to make a heart
    and lie down in the heart,

let horse flies plant
    hearts in our heads.

Dancer

When I become a tree where is the centre of this decision?
At the tip of each root, the tip of each branch –
my brain is millions of buds picked out against the air,

I am a shape of chemical channellings, electrical lengths,
impenetrable and porous. I bow to this:
we are gathered and flocked, I am a child forever –

I drop and redress my hair, I drop my hands and I raise them
to my mother. I remember the heart-cold and dry bands of heat
and I open my body as a cone, each fingernail fanning from its core.

Bunch

sunflower

stuffed his face with seed
gouty, corpulent, no space for dissent
or his teeth will fall out

daisy

white slips falling
gold at the heart
(also the making of all colours)
fine white slips
tipping her tongue

pansy

violet seam
bruised cuffs
three faces in a little hood

lily

dragging her bedsheets
and weeping behind –
   pollinated bride

tulip

hold me up
black eye at the bottom of my cup

eggs and bacon (trefoil)

lift her literal hood
smell your breakfast cooking
   glorious hobo

meadowsweet

crowned, that
tipping summer –

bow, bow down,
torn beauty

hogweed

croned in the quartered air,
dancer flinging herself against the glass

the relief of letting arms fall
to sinuate as leaf or leaf-fall

seed

a quiet host, dun and courteous,
missive from the plant's dropped light,
thin coin with the light through –
I give it to nothing and no one.
the word is honesty

Songbird

Darkling, I listen, and for many a time
I am half in love with my own tenderness.
I cannot see what flowers are at my feet.

I turn to my body, often causing tears –
could you touch me here, very softly, please?
The grass, the thicket and the fruit-tree wild,

a sweet clear voice is falling from my mouth
and I am already half in love with you –
real bird, collar of feathers lifting –

such air displaced by your body,
tender touch across my own small body –
the coming musk-rose, full of dewy wine.

I hold your voice lightly in my throat,
no space in the note but itself –
oh, touch my body tenderly. Yes, the tone

like an egg, line-less and unbroken –
our throats skinned-open and trembling,
I touch myself, the weight of living bird.

Instrumental

still others require song to have syllabic diversity   the repetitive and transformative
patterns that define music   which songs are songs   and which are calls
some groups are nearly voiceless almost all song is sung by male birds
babblers, the scimitar babblers some owls occupy an acoustic niche
the available frequency range is partitioned   music reflects some
pre-ordained harmony we can all sing we can all draw   when
I hear some   harmonies I break down   I feel the weave
all the chancers   I am not afraid the birds   go on singing
banal and profound wind riffing their breasts the surge
to open their mouths louder and at a higher pitch
in urban zones along the roadside there is
a violent thrush I love it like my sons
young birds learn outlines of songs
from their fathers their mothers
are filling holes with flesh
seeds over generations
birds   form dialects
research on parrots
suggests   nouns
adjectives verbs
can we recover
vocal plasticity
indulge   us
bickering
uprising
wings

Birdsong

Into the marshes, flooded pits, blackthorn. Easy to dream the
Gothic lure, self-conscious isolate —

Into a weave of song, just as I hoped – small brown bird
turns his song —

Iterations, overhangs, most inward layer turned outward,
unrolling its linear & intently playing itself out of pattern —

The syrinx, its sleek double-fluting —

Into the nightingales at intervals, deep in thorn & each sings
differently, spilling,

I reach for my phone, present it to the air as if I can absorb
some —

[Male birds; I think of the females listening, wonder if they
feel safe as I wonder if I do or do not care —]

Into mutability, something held back between the pools & the
working river & it lets me half in, I sit with rabbits to eat —

The soft call of the cuckoo, a packet of caterpillars loosens;
dozens writhe on leaves, lifting their ends as if testing the
spring air —

Turn on my phone & listen to nightingales in my room, hear
them with a sense of grief & I don't know where to place it

[Sparrows peck at mortar]

Blackbird takes his post, another answers, & another, until
these lines are wrung & we wetten & we falter —

Common Orange Lichen

Racy, flaky
           fry-up on the roof —
      mustard, Irn-Bru,
           hammered out in rusty truce.

How do you bear it?

Mulish, mulish,
           mottled underparts like bark,
so choral I would like to join your choir.

Flight

If love was like clouds and I leapt
from the plane, could I fall into you?
Could you bear me softly like faith,

muss my shadow with woolly devotion,
fold me into your core, where I could not feel
the rush of grave air?
Would you blind me, temporarily, please?

Let me glean this when I unbuckle, head for the exit:
your turning mass like milk in the belly
your lack of certainty, the way your edges furl –

Or let me make my own cloud
here on the pane – let me hush you into an oval window
wipe a line through my breath with a finger
as if proving I have agency over love, and water and air.

The Field

was once moor – purplish and peaty. Women bent over it, into the ground, picking shoots. They were shawled and stooped, low and ardent. They did not move with desperation but there was purpose in their going. A buzzard tilted, a lark folded in the machair. Rain came, quickly and violently wetting, and moved over.

The women went on, knowing their backs would dry.

A man stood in the hayrack, a bundle of grass in his arms. There were shouts as he hoisted thickets, tossed them to other men, bundling and tying. The scent of cut grass, cut with urine, smelt like elderflower. The man threw down a morsel – a field mouse, a shrew, to the cat.

There were strains of melody as women tended a pot, stirring and chopping. Stirring was for the most fearsome-appearing of the women; her face was clouds moving over a puddle. A child went at a root with a flint. A baby wailed for milk. The first pipistrelles emerged like small dark gossips never repeated. A boy pushed at the tick bite on his calf, there was a dog's hoarse bark.

The next time I went a man was waiting by the thick cob wall of the barn. The top floor had gone and space yawned into the roof. Someone had fixed an owl box high, at an angle. Underneath were tarry pellets. The man knelt down and broke open a large pellet with his fingers. It opened easily, like bread. Inside were tufts of fur and bones. He slid them across his finger pads, letting the dust fall finely. In his hands was a humerus.

The owls shifted in their box, talons hard against the grain.

Another man, now. This one has a waterproof coat and a gun across his back. He is grey-skinned, strong across the planes of his body. He climbs over the stile into the field and crosses it, diagonally. A roe deer starts and is away before the man sees her. He smells the scent of her going. A tractor grinds its gears.

And here is a woman, running   Or is it the deer again? Always the beat of blood, drawn through the earth. A child goes at a root with a flint. A baby wails for milk. An engine grinds its gears.

Violets

endlessly, what is death?

                    two bare trees like lungs

      no voices here
but violets — how bright they are, how intimate

*

each body fruits   young girls

                  turning cartwheels, chests smooth,
wrists small
un-damnable hearts

                why do we cry so?
see how the days fill our arms with flowers

*

shivering and gathering their spring accents now

goat-faced with pale spurs
I think they are reeling

            faint lines of scent

  each petal a gift and a loss

              the growing and the gone,
darling violets

bring me fresh violets   wet from the fields
stuff my mouth with their heart leaves
lay them over my shattered eyes,

          cover my body with flowers

little mothers, they cosset   fussing, softly,
into the dark

The Turn

Under the tree
I touch the earth and it is hot.
Figures watch, big-eyed.
The tree throws down its mast.
So many flying things in the air
sings my body,
Yankee Doo— sings the ice cream man,
red mouth opening upward.
The year is passing, golden and tiring.
Something is always fiercely opening.
        In and out of the retinal mind
I wind down with a red kite,
the toll of its body over the tyred way.
The horizon comes forward,
the dead joining the dead.
An upright man passes in bright cloth.
A bulbed mind draws lines
over sand or paper or skin.
A gourd thins and thickens with light.
A pause.
The sun is a small word.
In this way the turn withstood itself.
In this way I set toward the tree, one layer of carbon.

Inconsolable Green

Green the touched wood –

pods, tongues,
                 soft green explosions.

Green the hood, the egg, the gut –

an old eye,
green the pelt, green the snails,
green the weed between the words,
                              green the green sidle to heaven

(ear to the hide, hearts stowed)

                    *

Green the mall –

every cocked finger,
green wiped down the sides and in the cubicles
harkening, kneeling –

                    *

Greenly we come   the truth to green,
                 looped breath, perpetual singing –

Nothing but the gumming green,
up through the teeth

green bells beckoning –

Still green, polar green, some sick uprising,

sap, ichor, courage   unbiddable ghyll!

Dearest green, inconsolable green,
contrails spinning lime and mint-green light

green the crooning   croon the thrown song, now

Familial

I am outside, so often outside,
world moving through my body —
with my body I make these marks.

I breathe air, woodland air,
listen to recordings of extinct animal sounds.

Try tying knots into a poem or a person
to keep them slipping from your hand.
It can happen.

I breathe woodland rain, I believe it,
there is no seam to wood or family, or tree —
we climb sideways like fungi or dreams.

I reach my son's skin,
the mallow, the dog rose,
each small raging heart.

I look past me, then I look past me —

these lines the desire paths
an animal chose as it ran
its body through a world.

My grandmother is in the memory field.
Her paddock, her calves —
she pushes against gravity

up the hill, push push,
damp socks on the washing line.

Every day we wake and rise,
small, compressed animals
running over the bridge into the world.

Lemur

The sea is moving, people are falling over the edge
and newsprint dries in columns and fonts –

I dream a lemur in black and white, an aged lemur,
his dark coded tail   The weather is always changing;
we strive to keep up but lemur, darling, you live in my head
and that is enough. It is a tragedy when anything drowns.

The weather is inside me, blue skies in lemur country.
One day I might change the backdrop to my lemur
like orange or blue in a photo booth, draw the stringy curtain.
The words are trying to travel and I can't stay,

they unravelled that birthday at Bristol Zoo
when I reached double figures, a white bear rocked on a
plastic shore
and the penguins were not hungry.

The weather today is dutiful, behind me like a bad filter;
what if it changed like a mood ring?
It would mostly be purple and sullen.
Oh how beautiful are lime leaves against a thunderous sky
before the rain marks the earth in tiny pocks
The weather is exotic now, and local.

Tomorrow I will dig for acorns, like something precious,
which is what I'll call them.

Notes

'Apples'
'Language is a skin: I rub my language against the other.' –
Roland Barthes, *A Lover's Discourse*.

'Ring'
This tender little child gave up enough flesh to make a circlet
of ring. From the letters of St Catherine of Siena.
A little piece of skin alike the skin in an egg. From 13th-century
Agnes Blannbekin, to an anonymous scribe.
Wings of goldfinch. From a description of gamboge yellow in
Werner's nomenclature of colours, 1821.

'Desert Holly'
This poem adapts the titles of some projects by artist Martin
Roth, 1977–2019, whose work used living organisms in unusual
contexts.

'Iron Baby'
After the sculpture of the same name by Antony Gormley, 1999.

'Pigeons'
'Men still live who, in their youth, remember pigeons; trees still
live who, in their youth, were shaken by a living wind. But a few
decades hence only the oldest oaks will remember, and at long
last only the hills will know.' —Aldo Leopold, 'On a Monument
to the Pigeon', 1947.

'Fair Maids of February'
A folk name for the snowdrop.

'The Walled Garden'
A walled garden is a technical term for a restricted browsing environment on the internet and a 'closed ecosystem in which all the operations are controlled by the ecosystem operator' — Pierre de Poulpiquet, 2017.

'With a pure heart fervently'
Poem after 1 Peter 1:22 – 1:24 KJV.

'Small Rain'
A cento drawn from Gilbert White's diaries, most often from mid-March.

'Princess'
Sixty million flowers were laid down for the 'Queen of Hearts' at Kensington Palace.

'Songbird'
This poem responds to and uses some lines from Keats' 'Ode to a Nightingale'.

'Instrumental'
Some text in this poem uses text from the Wikipedia entry on bird vocalisation.

Acknowledgments

Thanks are due to the editors of the following publications where some of these poems first appeared: *Finished Creatures, Wild Court, Strix, SEISMA, Coast to Coast to Coast, Perverse, Back from the Brink, Rewilding, Ten poems about Clouds* (Candlestick Press), *The Utopia Project, Arrival at Elsewhere* (Against the Grain). 'Breast' won first prize in the Manchester Cathedral Poetry competition. Thank you to Bethan Roberts and Liverpool University Literature and Science hub for commissioning 'Songbird' in 2019 for A Nightingale Sang in Abercromby Square.

I am grateful to the Society of Authors and Arts Council England for grants that opened up time and space to write some of these poems. They have grown from the North Kent marshes, the London borough of Bexley and North Devon, amongst other places.

Thank you to all who helped breathe life into this collection: the Nevada Street Poets, Deryn Rees-Jones, Hannah Steen, and all at Pavilion Poetry, Judith Westcott for the drawings of spindles and nasturtium seeds, my family and the living, turning world.